giraffaroo

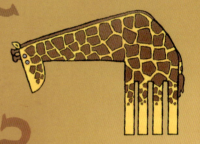

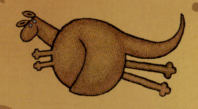

walmonkey

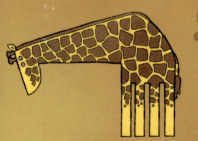

walion

camelgaroo

Lila Prap
Why?

Dear curious friends,
Some of the answers to the questions in this book are silly,
some are sensible, and some are scientific.
(Those are the ones marked by an asterisk ★.)
But feel free to make up some questions,
some answers, and some animals of your own.
They can be silly or serious ... whichever you like.

First American Edition 2005
by Kane/Miller Book Publishers, Inc.
La Jolla, California

Copyright © Mladinska knjiga Zalozbă, 2003

First published in Slovenia in 2003 under the title Zakaj? by Lila Prap
Mladinska knjiga
Slovenska cesta 29, 1000 Ljubljana Slovenia

All rights reserved.
For more information contact:
Kane Miller, A Division of EDC Publishing
P.O. Box 470663
Tulsa, OK 74147-0663
www.kanemiller.com
www.edcpub.com

Library of Congress Control Number: 2005923346
Printed and Bound in China by Regent Publishing Services, Ltd.

5 6 7 8 9 10 11 12 13 14

ISBN: 978-1-929132-80-5

Kane Miller
A DIVISION OF EDC PUBLISHING

Lila Prap

THEY HAVE A SCREW LOOSE.

Because they're childish.

I don't know.   It tickles them

Why do hyenas laugh?

★ They don't! But when excited or when being attacked, a spotted hyena will make a giggling noise that sounds like a person laughing. Even though hyenas are primarily predators (they kill their own food), they also like other animals' leftovers, such as bones, hooves and fur.

to walk barefoot on the grass.

THEY
ESCAPED
FROM
A PRISON.

Because their
mamas are
striped, too.

Because they can't

ZEBRAS ARE HORSES WEARING PAJAMAS.

★ Every zebra has a different and unique stripe pattern, just as every person has a different and unique fingerprint. Their stripes can be used to tell them apart, but many scientists believe their stripes also help to confuse predators.

decide whether to be black or white.

IT'S THEIR RUNNY NOSES!

To wash the clouds.

They're watering the sea grass.

WHY DO WHALES SPOUT WATER?

THEY ALWAYS HAVE COLDS.

★ Whales don't spout water, but from a distance it might look as if they do. When whales go under water they hold their breath. When they come to the surface of the water, they blow the moist air out their nose – the blowhole on top of their head. Scientists can sometimes tell the type of whale by the size and shape of the mist!

For fun.

TO FOLLOW THEIR NOSES.

So they

They wouldn't grow anywhere else.

So we can grab them if they want to run away.

WHY do rhinos have

★ Rhinoceros use their horns for fighting and for protection. Some species of rhinos have one horn, and some have two. The rhino is not as tough as it looks. Rhinos can't sweat, and their skin doesn't protect them from insects. Wallowing in the mud cools them off and keeps the bugs away.

horns on their noses?

WHY DO CAMELS HAVE

Because it's better than not having any.

They didn't sit up straight when they were little.

They aren't humps; they're sand dunes

HUMPS? TO CONFUSE THEIR RIDERS.

Out of habit.

★ Camels are perfectly suited to life in the desert. They store fat in their humps for times when food and water are scarce. The hump is able to provide energy for up to a week.

that camels carry across the desert.

They're afraid of water.

Because nobody wants

WHY do crocodiles cry?

They cry when they're sleepy.

★ Crocodiles are not sad, and they don't really cry, but they do like to lie in the sun. Their eyes can dry out when they are not in the water, and the tears help to keep their eyes wet and comfortable.

to play with them.

Because they swallowed

They like having their heads in the clouds.

Because their bodies are slower.

uncooked spaghetti.

I have no idea.

★ Thanks to both their long necks and their long tongues, giraffes can eat their favorite thorny acacia leaves which grow high above the grasslands. Their keen eyesight, together with their height, also makes it easier to spot predators lurking far away.

WHY DO GIRAFFES HAVE LONG NECKS?

To
put
their
toys
in.

So they don't lose their

pouches? **To hide their bellybuttons.**

Because.

★ Only female kangaroos have pouches – places for their babies to finish growing. When baby kangaroos, called joeys, are born they're very tiny, about the size and weight of a jellybean! The joey stays in its mother's pouch, drinking her milk for many months before it's big enough to venture out and eat the plants and grasses that grown-up kangaroos enjoy.

babies when they jump.

So the doctor can check their tonsils.

They're

Who knows?

They're bored.

WHY

sunning their teeth.

★ When hippos open their mouths wide, it looks like they're yawning, but really they're challenging someone to a fight! Hippos might seem slow and gentle, but they can be very aggressive, very dangerous, and very fast. They feed mostly at night, coming on land to eat plants and grasses. In one night, a hippo can eat up to 100 pounds of grass.

DO HIPPOS YAWN?

Why do lions have manes?

To know
where
their
head is.

Because they eat the barbers

So they aren't mistaken for cows.

To show off.

★ Manes help to make lions look bigger, stronger and scarier. Manes also protect the lions' necks during fights. Only male lions have manes, which start to grow when they're about two years old.

who try to trim their hair.

Because they'd hate cutting their toenails.

So they don't have to play football.

So they don't fall

don't snakes have legs?

They
forgot to
grow them.

★ Snakes don't need legs! They are able to use their muscles and spine to slide along on their bellies in an S-shaped pattern. Some kinds of snakes do have barely visible vestigial legs though, which are non-functioning.

down.

TO TICKLE BABIES.

They don't know how to shave.

DO WALRUSES HAVE

To look handsome.

To hide their big mouths.

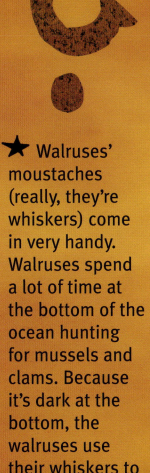

★ Walruses' moustaches (really, they're whiskers) come in very handy. Walruses spend a lot of time at the bottom of the ocean hunting for mussels and clams. Because it's dark at the bottom, the walruses use their whiskers to comb the mud, gravel and sand for their food.

MOUSTACHES?

WHY

To have
a swinging
time.

To be
different.

To tie themselves to

★ New World monkeys from Mexico, Central America and South America, have prehensile tails — tails that can grab and hold things. Old World monkeys living in Asia, the Middle East and Africa use their tails mostly for balance.

trees on windy days.

Because they are nosy.

No reason.

To store snot.

WHY DO ELEPHANTS HAVE

To trumpet their goodbyes.

★ An elephant's trunk is its nose, but it does much more than smell. It's also used for drinking (actually blowing water into the mouth), communicating, feeding, fighting, touching, lifting, greeting, throwing dust, and just about anything else you can think of. It is both strong enough to push down trees and nimble enough to pick up a single piece of straw.

TRUNKS?

WHO IS WHO:

Lila Prap
Pictures and text

Jelka Pogačnik
Scientific explanations

Lili Potpara
English translation

I don't like any of the answers!

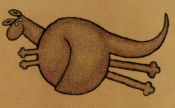

giraffamel

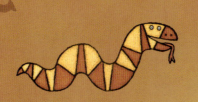

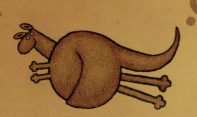

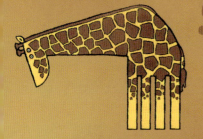

monklion

walyena

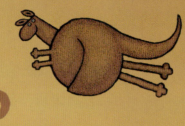

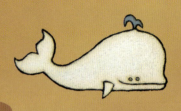

snakegaroo